POWER

OF

DISCIPLINE

Keys to Unstoppable Productivity and Success

THE
CORNERSTONE
PUBLISHING

TIMOTHY O. ABRAHAM

POWER OF DISCIPLINE

Keys to Unstoppable Productivity and Success

Copyright © 2018 by **Timothy O. Abraham**

ISBN: 978-1-944652-58-6

Cornerstone Publishing
A Division of Cornerstone Creativity Group LLC
Phone: +1(516) 547-4999
info@thecornerstonepublishers.com
www.thecornerstonepublishers.com

To order bulk copies of this book or to contact the author please call or (832)-287-2492
email: abrolus555@gmail.com

DEDICATION

I gracefully dedicate this book to God Almighty, for His mercy and loving kindness in my life.

I thank Him for His grace to write this book. Hallelujah!

DEDICATION

I gracefully dedicate this book to God Almighty, for His mercy and loving kindness in my life.

I thank Him for His grace to write this book. Hallelujah!

CONTENTS

INTRODUCTION

I want to thank you for getting this book, 'The Power of Discipline: Key to Unstoppable Productivity & Success."

Most of us hate rules! When we hear the word 'discipline,' we are automatically reminded of convents and boot camps. Who doesn't love living each day, as it goes, without any rules? Of course, there are joys that can be experienced by living a carefree life! But if you want a life filled with happiness, that can be sustained, you need to bring in some rules!

And there is no necessity that rules are always bad. You won't believe how incorporating discipline as part of your life can help you improve the quality of your life and sustain your happiness! I encourage you to not be immediately put off by the idea of adding some discipline to your life. I am sure that this book will give you a fresh perspective on discipline and help you realize how it improves your life! Hence, I strongly urge you to stay patient until you finish this book. Your patience will duly be rewarded!

The first chapter of this book deals with the art of discipline and how it is an important ingredient for achieving success. The second chapter highlights the various benefits of incorporating discipline as part of your life. The third chapter stresses on how lack of discipline can damage your life. The fourth chapter focuses on strategies or tips that can help you incorporate self-discipline. The fifth chapter of this book talks about famous celebrities, who have incorporated discipline as part of their lives. Finally, the sixth chapter throws light on why self-disciple is better and more important than motivation.

I hope you find this book useful and interesting! Thank you for purchasing this book.

Chapter 1

THE ART OF DISCIPLINE

Through this chapter, I hope to throw more light on what discipline entails, especially what discipline and self-discipline is all about and how it can help you to achieve success.

WHY DO WE NEED DISCIPLINE?

We are part of a generation, which likes living each day on its own terms. We shy away from rules and aspire to live each moment to its fullest, without any restraint. While this might not sound too bad, have you ever wondered why you didn't get into the college that you wanted? Or get that job you coveted the most? Have you ever thought why you find it difficult to sustain your relationships? Have you always been puzzled as to why your results are never commensurate to the amount of effort that you put in? The answer to these above questions could be the lack of discipline. The reason why some of us fail to meet our targets, despite our best efforts, is because we lack the discipline. Again, as I said before, do not look at discipline as a negative element of your life.

Let me give you an example to prove how discipline is important for even following your passions! Let's assume that you are part of your school's basketball team. You have an important tournament coming up in a month. Luckily, all your fellow players are in good form and are extremely talented. Is this enough to get you that trophy? No. You must practice every day for a certain number of hours. You will have to practice your routine several times. Even if your strategy for this game is the same and you have played your opponent several times in the past to understand their style, you still need to practice. Why are you indulging in so much practice? To ensure that your body is in good form and to mentally prepare yourself for the game! Isn't this a form of disciplining your body and mind?

Out of passion for winning, all of you come together and engage in so much practice! All of you may have different playing styles. But it is extremely important that your styles are aligned on the day of the game, to reap the maximum benefits. It is discipline that brings you together as a team. You will see in a while how discipline/self-discipline will help you achieve success!

Living with no regrets is a good thing. But living, without worrying about consequences, is bad and detrimental to not just you but to the people around you as well. Most of us don't really see how our actions impact others. We fail to appreciate the importance of the things that we have. This is one important reason why this generation are pros at procrastination. We would rather spend hours on Snapchat or Twitter or Instagram, instead of focusing on the work at hand. You will be able to get away with this reckless attitude only while the consequences aren't too severe. But why wait until things get out of hand to do course corrections? When you are disciplined, you will surely be cognizant of your actions and behaviors.

WHAT IS DISCIPLINE?

Now that I have spent quite some time talking about discipline, let's see what it refers to. Discipline is nothing but the practice of getting trained or conditioned to think or react in a certain way, within a certain framework of principles. Sounds boring and daunting? Well, let us look at what self-discipline is all about. You will probably realize that discipline is not about a life based on someone else's rules. It's about having your own set of rules and living your life based on that!

WHAT IS SELF-DISCIPLINE?

Self-discipline is nothing but the ability to control one's thoughts, actions, emotions and behaviors. With self-discipline, you will be able to control your impulsive reactions. By exercising self-discipline, you are consciously letting go of the need to be immediately gratified or upset by your surroundings! It is a conscious effort to hold back your emotions and not react immediately. In other words, self-discipline is all about being in control of your life and reaping the maximum benefits from it.

When I say that you need discipline in your life, it does not mean that you should let go of your happiness and lead a boring life! You can continue having fun and do all the things that you like, so long as they are not detrimental to your overall wellbeing (ex: drug addiction). In fact, you will realize that having a bit of discipline can improve the quality of your relationships and help you sustain your happiness. Hence, it is not a bad thing after all. Self-discipline is all about improving your focus, directing your efforts in a more effective manner and reaping the maximum benefits from all your undertakings!

INGREDIENT FOR SUCCESS

Self-discipline plays an important role in helping you achieve success in whatever you do. It helps you hit the mark in the following manner:

When you are disciplined, your tolerance levels are increased. Hence, you end up persevering more. You will not be easily disturbed by situations, which may put you out of your comfort zone. When your perseverance increases, you will keep going at your goal, no matter how many obstacles are placed on your way.

Discipline automatically tunes your mind to keep trying, despite failures. We all know that it is not possible to strike gold at the first attempt. With some patience and consistent efforts on your part, you will most certainly taste the fruits of success. Self-discipline equips you with the required patience.

Discipline helps you stay focused on your target. When you are focused, you will be in a better position to put in your best efforts. Discipline also helps you deal with distractions. You will not be easily distracted by things around you and will be able to focus on your target.

Another important quality required for chasing success is the ability to maintain a calm and composed head all the time. Discipline will help you achieve that! When your mind is not clouded by other impulsive thoughts, emotions or opinions, it becomes that much easier for you to focus.

These are some of the top reasons, which indicate that discipline/self-discipline is required for achieving success. The various benefits of self-discipline are highlighted in the upcoming chapter, for you to fully appreciate its importance.

GETTING STARTED

Including discipline into your life is not an unpleasant experience, contrary to popular belief. It is all a matter of perspective. You can look at discipline as a set of rules and dismiss it, only to regret it later. Or you can look at it as an opportunity to align your life with your goals, aspirations and passions!

Again, don't try to change your life all at once, under the pretext of disciplining it. Make incremental changes to your thought processes and your routines and see how it goes. Make course corrections, as and when required. Also, don't try to incorporate discipline as part of your life, in a rushed manner. Nothing good ever comes out of doing things in haste. To help you get started, I have provided a separate chapter detailing tips to incorporate discipline as part of your life. So, don't break your head too much yet, about disciplining your life.

I am sure that by the end of this book, you will realize that disciplining your life adds a lot of positivity to the various spheres of your life.

Chapter 2

BENEFITS OF SELF-DISCIPLINE

❧❧❧

Practicing self-discipline can most certainly help you alter your life in so many ways! It can improve the quality of the various spheres of your life, at the same time. Some of the top benefits of self-discipline are as follows:

HELPS IN ACHIEVING SUCCESS

As we have already seen, discipline is extremely crucial for achieving success in whatever you do! Being self-disciplined helps you channel your time and effort in the most constructive manner possible. You would be surprised by how much you can get done in a short span of time, if your efforts are channeled in a systematic manner! You will also be able to better manage your time, when you learn to discipline your mind!

IMPROVES YOUR PERSONALITY

When you include the practice of self-discipline into your life, your persona will change gradually. You will no longer be the lazy and carefree person you were! You will weigh each option more carefully and ensure that you are completely focused on what you are doing. This will automatically improve your productivity at work! When your productivity is rewarded, you will automatically feel more confident. Your outlook will become more and more positive. Hence, if you were someone with low self-esteem and low confidence levels, inculcating the practice of self-discipline will certainly help you improve these.

YOU WILL START BELIEVING IN YOURSELF!

When you discipline your mind, you will be able to channelize your efforts in a systematic manner. When your efforts are directed in an efficient manner, you will be able to accomplish a lot. When you are able to see your efforts translating into results, you will feel a sense of accomplishment. You will start believing in yourself more. You will trust yourself to see a task to its completion. Your confidence levels will improve tremendously and will have a positive effect on the quality of your work as well!

HELPS IN IMPROVING RELATIONSHIPS

On the personal front, when you are disciplined, you will be more balanced as a person. This will ensure that you don't immediately react to a situation, without deliberating about the pros and cons of each decision. Your conversations with others also will be more measured! You will be trusted by others to stay calm and take an informed decision. This trust removes unnecessary troubles or misunderstandings in your relationships with others. When your reactions are controlled, the chances of you wreaking havoc in a relationship are slim. Hence, you will be able to improve your relationships by practicing self-discipline!

IMPROVES YOUR MENTAL CLARITY

As I mentioned before, when you practice self-discipline, you will be able to exuberate calmness in all situations. You will tackle any situation in a systematic manner. This automatically improves your mental clarity. How so? Let's assume that you are in a chaotic situation. When your mind is not disciplined, you will be all over the place. There will be thousands of thoughts crossing your mind at the same time. You may end up reacting, without actually thinking it through! Your mind will be clouded by the emotions and anxiety and you wouldn't be able to think straight. On the other hand, when your mind is disciplined, you will be able to assess the situation in a calm and composed manner.

You will approach the situation in hand in a systematic manner by breaking it down into smaller components. This will help you take better decisions. Hence, without a doubt, self-discipline improves your mental clarity and your ability to make sound decisions.

HELPS YOU APPRECIATE LIFE BETTER

As I said before, your attitude changes when you discipline your mind. When your outlook turns positive, you will learn to appreciate life better. You will start seeing the silver lining in any situation. You will start being grateful for the various things around you. This is possible only when you are calm and composed and have a positive mindset. All this comes hand in hand with self-discipline!

When you learn to appreciate even the smallest of things around you, you will be able to find happiness in whatever you do! You don't need external stimuli to keep you happy. You will feel contented and happy, even when the odds are stacked against you. This also adds on to your mental clarity!

HELPS YOU LET GO OFF YOUR ADDICTIONS!

Self-discipline is extremely crucial when you are trying to mend your ways and get rid of your bad habits, especially addictions! Unless you learn to control your mind, you will not be able to resist the bad habits. For instance, if you are trying to fight off procrastination, you need to discipline your mind first. This is because procrastination has got more to do with your lazy mindset. The sooner you discipline your mind, the sooner will you be able to limit your tendencies to procrastinate.

Hence, disciplining your mind is the first step before you attempt to let go off any habits. When your mind is disciplined, you don't need external motivation to stick to your schedule.

INCULCATING GOOD HABITS!

Self-discipline need not apply to just letting go off addictions. Self-discipline is important even for incorporating good habits and practices. For instance, if you are trying to get on a diet, you need self-discipline to stick to the diet, no matter how tempted you are to eat out. Similarly, when you are trying to get on an exercise regime, you need the discipline to get on with your schedule every day! Disciplining provides a sense of direction, which can help you stay on track!

CONTROL YOUR STRESS LEVELS

When you learn to discipline your mind, you will most certainly be able to regulate your stress levels, owing to the following reasons:

You will not panic, at the outbreak of any situation. You will assess it with a calm and patient mind. This way, you are not reacting to the problem in hand immediately. This is vital for preventing you from acting out of impulse. This will automatically regulate your stress levels. In fact, there will be fewer things that will stress you out!

With self-discipline, you will be able to practice meditation regularly. This is another way of regulating your stress levels easily.

When you introduce self-discipline, you will be able to approach any situation with renewed positivity. This positivity will help you find solutions to your problems quicker and thus help you reduce your stress levels accordingly.

Thus, self-discipline will definitely improve your mental health, by not just regulating your stress levels but also by keeping your mind calm.

INCREASED ENERGY LEVELS

When you are disciplined, both physically and mentally, you will not be spending your energy on things not worth your time! When you channel your energies in the most productive manner, you will accomplish a lot within a given period of time. This will give you a sense of accomplishment as well as motivation. This motivation is enough to sustain your energy levels for a longer duration of time.

Similarly, when you engage in healthy habits, such as healthy eating and regular exercise, you will be able to increase your energy levels easily. Another contributing factor towards sustaining your energy levels is that you will seldom waste your energy, fretting about issues. You will prefer to spend the time and energy on figuring out the issue in a calm and composed manner!

LEAD A HEALTHY LIFE

Self-discipline can improve the quality of your health in the following ways:

You will finally be prepared to let go off the dirty habits which are impacting your health.

You will be in a better position to practice healthy habits regularly and reap the complete benefits.

You will also be able to improve your mental health, by reducing your stress levels and keeping a cool head!

With self-discipline, you will be able to stick to the course of your treatment, without any deviations. This will help in accelerating your recovery, when you fall sick.

Your immunity levels are also improved, when you consciously pay attention to what you eat and how you burn off your extra calories!

When you discipline your mind, you no longer have to worry about not falling asleep at night. With reduced stress levels and a calm mind, you will be able to fall asleep the minute you hit the bed. You will also be able to get in the requisite amount of sleep (7 to 8 hours). Sleeping enough is extremely important for leading a healthy lifestyle.

As you can see, the benefits of self-discipline are countless. The above benefits are merely illustrative. You may experience various other benefits, as a result of practicing self-discipline.

POWER OF DISCIPLINE

It is important you practice discipline, if you aspire to grow professionally as well as on the personal front and lead a healthy lifestyle.

Chapter 3

WHY POOR DISCIPLINE CAN DESTROY YOU

I am sure you will have realized by now, that the benefits of self-discipline are countless. To motivate you to practice self-discipline, here are some important effects of lack of discipline. You will be surprised to see how lack of discipline can affect the quality of your life, in so many ways.

ON THE PATH TO SELF-DESTRUCTION!

When we are not disciplined, it simply means that we are going to be victims of our problems and bad habits. Bad habits turn into addictions, which ultimately consume our happiness, peace and health. Nothing good ever comes out of succumbing to an addiction. What follows suit will be a list of things to be worried about. You will feel remorseful for being an addict but, at the same time, feel miserable for not being able to resist your urges. You will get sucked into the vortex of misery and depression and getting through each day is going to be a tougher ordeal!

SELF-INTEREST

When you are not disciplined, it will be very hard for you to appreciate what you have. You will end up craving for more and putting your interests above others.' Your efforts will mostly be channelized towards achieving only your desires, without taking into consideration the welfare of others. The simple fact that you are indulging in your addictions to derive happiness, knowing pretty well how it will impact your friends and family, is an indication that you value your own interests more than that of others.' This will not only hamper your relationships with others but also have an impact on your career. Nobody likes working with an individual who constantly puts his interests above the team's interests. Hence, it can have some jarring consequences on the work front as well.

LACK OF RESPONSIBILITY

When you are not disciplined, you seldom care about the consequences of your actions or inaction. Also, only a person, who is capable of putting others' interests above his'/hers, will be able to take the lead on things and assume responsibility. I have already mentioned how lack of discipline makes one selfish. This makes it even more difficult to assume responsibility, for matters concerning work as well as your personal life.

When you constantly shy away from taking responsibility for your actions, it has the following impacts:

You will not be respected by your peers or your superiors. After all, responsibility and accountability are extremely important, when working as a team. When you are always trying to pass on the baton, people would no longer care about passing it to you in the first place. Hence, this attitude will definitely affect your chances of a promotion.

On the personal front, it will increase the frustration levels of your friends and family members, when you are not taking responsibility for the various tasks at home or for your actions. Not even your loved ones will be interested to cut you some slack forever and take on the extra work. Hence, it is important that you don't ruin your existing relationships by shrugging off your responsibilities every time.

YOU FEEL AGITATED!

When your mind lacks discipline, it becomes that much more complicated to control your emotions and thoughts. When faced with an adversity, you will feel agitated and lose track of the solution. Your mind will be clouded with your impulsive thoughts, which will hamper your decision making as well.

Similarly, when you get addicted to your desires, it becomes difficult to get out of it, without disciplining your mind first. You may attempt getting out of the addiction, only to fail shortly. We have already seen how addictions are capable of destroying our happiness. Added to that, the loss of our loved ones' trust can also be quite discouraging. All these will certainly add on to your frustration and agitation.

YOU WILL BE CONSTANTLY CRITICIZED!

Of course, there will be a group of people, who will criticize, no matter how earnest and disciplined you are. I am not referring to that bunch, when I mean that you will be subject to constant criticism. Your colleagues, managers, even your own family will criticize you, owing to the following reasons:

When you lack discipline, your efforts will not be spent only for productive things. For instance, you would end up spending time and money on your addictions, which could have otherwise been utilized in a productive manner. This could affect your productivity at work as well as your personal relationships.

When your mind lacks discipline, you will always behave in an impulsive manner. However, this might not be the best way to deal with most problems in hand.

We have already seen how self-interest is an offshoot of lack of discipline. When you are forever putting your interests above that of others, it indicates that you are not a team player or someone, who is not vested in the interests of the family.

When you lack the discipline, you will end up defying authority, quite often, and not take responsibility either. People find it difficult to deal with individuals, who have a problem with the rules and yet do nothing to change the status quo.

LOW SELF-ESTEEM AND SELF-CONFIDENCE

When you realize that your efforts don't translate to results, you will automatically be frustrated. You will start questioning your ability to handle the task on hand. Gradually, your confidence levels and self-esteem will drop. You will not be motivated to do anything with full vigor. Abstaining from putting your best efforts will only result in more failures. Hence, it is a vicious cycle of disappointment.

Further, when you are constantly subject to criticism, you start losing trust in your abilities. You will also constantly be disappointed with your inability to get over your bad habits and addictions. This also affects your morale to a large extent.

PESSIMISM

Constant failures may impair your optimism to a large extent. Over time, you end up becoming cynical and looking at everything in a negative vein. You end up developing a pessimistic attitude. As a result, you will generalize your misfortunes and not focus on solving the problem in hand. You will fail to look at the obvious solutions staring at your face. You would rather spend your energy and time cribbing about your problems, than actually solving it.

This pessimistic attitude will have a grave impact on your professional development as well. Managers like rewarding people, who are solution providers. You will not be looking for the solutions in any situation, if you have a pessimistic mindset. In the absence of sufficient gratification at work, you will not be motivated to work better. On the personal front, your family and friends will refrain from sharing any problem with you, because you have nothing to offer, except your pessimism. This will also hamper your mental peace and happiness.

POOR HEALTH

Your health, both physical and mental, takes a huge toll on you, when you lack discipline. When you lack discipline, it simply translates to lack of respect for your body and mind! You will not pay attention to what you eat! You will not spend the time and effort to indulge in fitness activities. You find it extremely difficult to let go of your bad habits. This definitely has a bearing on your physical wellbeing. The more and more you get addicted to something, the more the quality of your health starts spiraling in a downward direction.

On the other hand, you also feel agitated and stressed quite often. As an offshoot of stress, you find it difficult to sleep peacefully. You may end up suffering from anxiety attacks. Hence, your mental health also goes for a toss, when you lack discipline.

LACK OF PRODUCTIVITY

When you are not disciplined, you will seldom have any respect for anything, including time. You won't think twice before you throw away your time on something unproductive. You will happily be a prisoner of procrastination. When you keep procrastinating constantly, you will realize that you have much less time left to focus on the deliverables in hand. You end up doing a botched job, by trying to finish everything at the last minute. When you meet all your deliverables at the last minute and in a rushed manner, the quality of your work is greatly compromised. You may end up reworking on most of your deliverables, to ensure that they are error free and meaningful. This is nothing but being unproductive. When you are not productive, it has an impact on your professional development.

When procrastination creeps to the other spheres of your life, your overall happiness will be gravely affected. For instance, if you forever put off making plans to meet a friend, you might end up losing that friendship. When you put off making important decisions, you may end up compromising the happiness of your family and friends as well. This will definitely impact the quality of your relationships with others. Similarly, when you put off following a certain diet always, you may end up compromising on the quality of your health as well.

Chapter 4

7 STRATEGIES TO BUILD UNBREAKABLE SELF-DISCIPLINE

❧❧❧

Now that you have a fair idea about the importance of self-discipline, it is time to get started. Here are some tips/strategies to help you build your self-discipline and get rewarded in the long run. A word of caution, you may not be able to implement these tips in the most perfect manner from day one itself. There will, of course, be some resistance while implementing these changes. Give it some time and be patient, you will definitely get there!

LEARN TO TAKE STOCK OF YOUR WEAKNESSES

Being aware of your pitfalls is the first step

towards tackling them. These can be in the form of bad habits, addictions or issues with your attitude. Ignoring your vices will not help you in any way to get disciplined. Just list them down. When you have an exhaustive list, you will be able to come up with ways to tackle them and discipline your mind in the process.

COME UP WITH AN ACTION PLAN

Now that you have come up with your list of weaknesses, think of ways to overcome them. There need not be only one solution to your addictions or weaknesses. List all possible solutions and see how you can implement them. Come up with a revised schedule for the next week, to see how these ideas fit in. Again, this does not have to be a perfect plan. You can also revisit this and tweak, to better address your weaknesses. Having a written plan will give you a sense of direction and purpose. It can also be a source of reinforcement, when you think that you are being tempted by your vices! Come up with a routine, based on your schedule. A daily routine can help you discipline your mind easily, over time!

For instance, if one of your weaknesses is addiction to social media, think of ways to handle it. If temporarily deactivating your account is an option, then go on and do it. If that's not feasible, come up with a plan to reduce the number of hours you spend on social media. If your schedule is filled with other activities, then you will invariably be left with less time for social media. Hence, increase the time that you spend outdoors.

STAY COMMITTED

It is not important if you just come up with a plan. It is important that you put it to action and stay committed to the plan. Here are some ways to ensure that your plan is put into action:

If there are any objects in your surroundings, which are capable of distracting you, remove them from your vicinity. If you are a TV/ Netflix addict, it could be as trivial as removing those posters of your favorite TV shows from your room. These posters can remind you of these shows and make you watch them. By removing them, you are controlling your addiction for watching TV shows.

Ensure that you are surrounded by positive reinforcements. For instance, if you are trying to reduce your tendencies to procrastinate, then make sure you have some post-it stickers on your table to remind you the importance of the deliverable or decision.

There are various scheduling apps available today, which can be used for going through each item on your agenda. You will also get a sense of accomplishment when you cross items off the list. These apps can also serve as a visual aid to help you stick to your schedule.

Have a sound reward system in place. I'll touch upon this aspect in a bit. Having a reward system will definitely motivate you to follow your plan effectively.

Come up with a list of non-negotiables. When you have a list of things that you can't compromise on, you will be disciplined to follow it, no matter what.

It is important that you learn to stick to your plan. By doing so, you are actually conditioning and disciplining your mind. Of course, it will be difficult to follow your plan initially. But, with patience and sufficient reinforcements, you should be able to stick to it easily.

LEARN TO PRIORITIZE

Not all of us are gifted with the ability to prioritize our tasks in an effective manner. This is not only with respect to our work, but also applies to our emotions. Hence, by practicing the art of prioritizing, you are disciplining your mind to look at important tasks first. For example, when your mind is disciplined, you will be able to approach a situation in a calm manner. You will not give priority to your impulsive reactions. You would only prioritize your solutions. So, learning to prioritize is important to discipline your mind and body. Having a written schedule or plan will help you spend time assessing and ranking these tasks, based on priority.

INCREASE YOUR TOLERANCE LEVELS

All of us like playing to our strengths and staying within our comfort zones. When we are asked to do something out of our comfort zone, we feel lost and struggle to complete it.

Hence, engage in activities which will make you step out of your comfort zone. This way, you will not be caught off guard later. By doing this, you are disciplining both your mind and body to stay composed, even when faced with a bizarre or an uncomfortable challenge in the future.

Similarly, do not run away from short-term discomforts because it might end up causing issues in the long run. Increase your tolerance for such discomforts. This will prepare your mind as well as your body for bigger challenges. Controlling your body and mind will not be an impossible task to begin with. For instance, if you don't want to suffer from the temporary discomforts of following a gym routine, you will end up facing health issues in the long run. If you accustom your body for a routine of 30 minutes, you will not find it difficult to increase the time to 45 minutes, if your physician so advises in the future. Hence, learn to prepare your body and mind for any kind of situation. When you anticipate anything, and are certain about the uncertainty, disciplining your mind amidst chaos won't be difficult.

COME UP WITH A SOUND REWARD SYSTEM

Disciplining your mind is not a joke at all. You will have to be patient and try continuously. This will ensure that you are able to get there someday. You might have to find ways to motivate yourself to stick to the plan. One easy way to ensure that you stay motivated is to have a sound reward system in place. This will ensure that you follow your plan, no matter what. Having a reward system in place helps you in the following ways:

For the longest of time, discipline has been considered as a form of punishment. This is one important reason why we consciously stay away from discipline. To eliminate that mental constraint, a reward system can definitely help. It can be used to recognize good and positive behavior or actions.

When there is a reward tagged to your schedule or plan, you would be motivated better to ensure that you complete your tasks on time. In a way, you will be channelizing your efforts and time towards the completion of the task.

Over time, you will be able to channelize your time and effort to words priority areas, without the need for a reward.

Rewards need not always be materialistic in nature. They can also be in the form of positive reinforcements. These can help in further disciplining your mind. For instance, your reward can be in the form of an evening out with your friends. These rewards can also be used to help you deal with your addictions. You would spend less time on social media, when you have an evening planned with your friend.

Here are some pointers to help you come up with a sound reward system:

Since the idea is to discipline your body and mind, it is extremely important that you choose the quantum of the reward in an appropriate manner. The reward that you choose should be in proportion with the target being set. For instance, if you are disciplining yourself to stay away from social media for three hours, do not come up with a reward allowing you to spend time outdoors for the entire weekend. If your reward is too much, your body or mind will not be disciplined in the process. On the other hand, if your reward is too less, you will not be motivated to discipline yourself.

It is extremely important that you time your rewards in an appropriate manner. For example, if you are testing a schedule for this week, make sure that you reward yourself, for following the schedule, during the weekend. If your reward is not timely, the purpose of having a reward in the first place is lost.

As I mentioned before, rewards can also be in the form of positive reinforcements. Rewards need not be entirely materialistic. When you choose an experience as a reward, you will learn more in the process.

Do not go for rewards, which are capable of affecting your resolve to discipline yourself. For example, you already know that you are addicted to social media. So, when you're deciding a reward for completing a certain college assignment, do not set it as spending 20 minutes on social media. By doing this, you are giving in to your temptations and reinforcing addictive behaviors.

Every time you come up with a plan to tackle your weaknesses and discipline yourself in the process, think about the rewards that come along with it. When I say rewards, I don't necessarily mean only the ones set by you. Think about the long-term benefits of disciplining yourself. Self-discipline can help you in numerous ways. Visualize your rewards, how your life can change for better, if you discipline yourself.

REVIEW YOUR PROGRESS

Just like how important it is to have a plan in place and execute it, it is equally important that you review your progress from time to time. You can choose the frequency of the review, depending on your motivation levels. For instance, if you are not so confident about your ability to stick to the plan, you can review on a daily or a weekly basis. On the other hand, if you are confident about your ability to follow the schedule, without many deviations, you can also go for a fortnightly or monthly review. Only when you review your progress, will you know if your ideas are working well.

This review process will help you make any changes to your plan, as and when required. You can also take the help of a friend or relative to be an independent reviewer and help you stay on track.

Chapter 5

HOW HIGHLY SUCCESSFUL PEOPLE DEVELOP POWERFUL SELF-DISCIPLINE

If there was one character trait that could assure success to a person, it would be self-discipline, followed closely by hard work. But you know what they say about hard work. It's not really about blind hard work but more about disciplined perseverance in the right direction that can help you become successful and achieve your goals.

In this part of the book, we are going to look closely into how self-discipline has quite possibly been the single most common trait among successful personalities from all walks of life. For this, I have singled out some eminent and highly accomplished individuals, who have contributed so much to their respective fields by their success. Their success stories have made their names synonymous with their profession/ industry. And mind you, I won't be doing a subjective analysis of how they excelled in their chosen field, but rather objectively assess how self-discipline has helped them become what they are today and how much they value self-discipline.

These chosen individuals belong to the world of politics, business, sports, technology and entertainment from the different parts of this world. All this just goes on to further underline the significance of having self-discipline and how it is, without doubt, one of the biggest assets you can have regardless of your profession or area of expertise. So, let us begin!

ARNOLD SCHWARZENEGGER

This man, quite literally, is one of the biggest advocates of self-discipline and hard work. He has explained on countless occasions on how he owes his achievements to self-discipline and commitment. He was one of the most decorated bodybuilders; hands down, one of the biggest bankable stars in Hollywood, when he was an actor full-time; a well-loved governor of the state of California, the Governator, as he was fondly called; he excelled in every challenge he took on.

In numerous videos and articles, Mr. Schwarzenegger has stressed on how self-discipline was the single most important aspect in his journey. It is quite easy to observe the benefits of self-discipline, in the context of his career as a professional bodybuilder. The sport requires total commitment towards the cause and self-discipline is the link that holds everything together. The fact that he won more titles during his career than a lot of his competitors put together, just goes on to show that his sense of self-discipline indeed was very high.

And his success story does not end there. After retiring from professional bodybuilding, Mr. Schwarzenegger pursued a career in Hollywood, and in that process, faced a new set of challenges. Being an immigrant and new to acting, he had to deal with a good amount of prejudice and outright rejection. But he persevered and slowly, with his hard work and sense of self-discipline, became one of the biggest action movie stars. Schwarzenegger went on to prove to the world that restrictions exist only as challenges to be broken, when he made his next career shift and moved to politics. Here again, his commitment, perseverance and self-discipline took him to the highest public office, an immigrant can hold in the United States – that of the Governor and he held the post of Governor of the State of California for multiple terms.

JACK MA

If there is one name that is synonymous with the current age of Internet based business models, it is that of Jack Ma. Born Ma Yun, this Chinese business mogul is the founder and head of Alibaba, a conglomerate of various businesses that have their founding on the Internet. Frequently making it to the list of top 5 most influential business icons of our generation, Jack Ma's story of success has its base in his strong sense of self-belief and self-discipline, even in the face of multiple rejections and failures.

His beginnings were more than just humble.

Right out of school, he struggled a lot to gain admission to college. He took 3 attempts to pass the entrance exams to his Alma Mater. Fresh out of college, he applied for 30 different jobs and unbelievably, got rejected by every single one of them. In fact, he even applied to Harvard 10 times, facing rejection every single instance. As you can clearly see, he was someone whose self-belief and perseverance knew no limits. His initial few business ventures also ended up as failures before he hit gold with the online marketplace that he started and the rest, as they say, is history.

Friends and acquaintances close to Jack Ma say that throughout his life, he has been an avid practitioner of meditation and the Chinese martial art form called Tai Chi, which is more a practice of self-discipline than anything else. In fact, Ma himself has praised the virtues of Tai Chi, doing his part in spreading awareness on the benefits of this martial art form and expressed his desire to be known as a practitioner and teacher of Tai Chi than an Internet business mogul. He is another excellent example of an individual, who fought against all odds and challenges, thanks to his strong sense of discipline.

SERENA & VENUS WILLIAMS

Any list of successful people would be incomplete without a mention of the Williams sisters. They have truly made a mark for themselves in tennis through their achievements and become cultural icons, standing as a source of inspiration to millions of people across the globe. Every aspect of their life and game is awe inducing and the only key to their achievements besides their skills, are their sheer hard work and self-discipline.

Playing a highly demanding sport at the age of 35 and 36, Serena and Venus are re-writing history every moment they set foot on a court. They have been tasting success continuously on a game, which is ironically infamous for burning out even world class athletes in even their twenties, due to the physical toil it demands. And the very fact that these sisters have not given up yet is astounding and inspiring.

Between the two of them, the Williams sisters hold a humongous 30 Grand Slam titles and that is not counting the Olympic medals and Doubles and Mixed Doubles titles. It can be said, without a doubt, that the game of tennis has never been the same since the Williams sisters made their debut. And they continue to dominate their games at this age, when their adversaries would have long retired. Overcoming extreme physical injuries and illnesses (Venus has been diagnosed with Sjogren's Syndrome and Serena has been plagued by knee and back injuries) and refusing to bow down to cultural and gender inequalities, they have made it clear, on multiple occasions, that they owe all their success to the countless hours of hard work and self-discipline behind each game. Often hitting the court before the sun is up; it is indeed their sheer dedication to the sport and extreme amounts of discipline in practice, which has given them the honor of being real game changers in the world of tennis.

MICHAEL PHELPS

With an all-time record of 28 Olympic medals to his name, 23 of which are gold, Michael Phelps is the highest decorated Olympian to date and arguably the greatest athlete as well. And beneath the aura of success and achievements is the man, who by his own admission once went five years without taking a single day off from training and the rigorous schedule of a competitive athlete. That is 1825 continuous days of hard work and practice! And if that is not the very definition of self-discipline and commitment, I can't quite imagine what else could be.

Phelps has been described by his coach, on multiple occasions, as someone who complements his extraordinary sporting abilities with insane levels of focus and commitment. His rigid and unwavering focus and determination has been praised by his teammates and foes alike. His almost obsessive pursuit of perfection has been often reported in the media and he truly lives up to it. He is said to have trained for up to 8 hours every day, without missing a single training day and spends the rest of the time resting and meditating. All this for a man, who admittedly suffers from ADHD, is indeed awe-inspiring. It again goes to prove that being intrinsically gifted with a certain skill can take you to great heights, only if those skills are complemented with hard work, self-discipline and perseverance.

WARREN BUFFET

Warren Buffet holds the official title of the CEO and Chairman of Berkshire Hathaway Inc. and unofficially he is known as the greatest and the most successful investors of our times. With huge stakes in many of the biggest public firms in the world, Buffet is considered to be an investment wizard by the financial sector. Often asked about the secret to his success, Buffet has attributed it to prudential investment tactics and self-discipline, which has helped him choose wisely and reap the maximum benefits from his investments. Exercising discipline in financial matters is extremely crucial for sustaining financial stability and he has proven it over the years!

Known to be a man who invests in a company rather than just its stock, Buffet has earned wide respect and admiration for his disciplined and humble life style in the backdrop of his billionaire status. On many occasions and forums, he has spoken about the importance of self-discipline and honest hard work as the key ingredients to success in the business world.

I hope these success stories motivate you to start disciplining your mind and body.

Chapter 6

THE SUPERIORITY
OF DISCIPLINE OVER
MOTIVATION

⁂

Finally, it is important that you understand why being disciplined is more important than being motivated. To simply put, being disciplined can impact your life in a more effective manner than being motivated.

Let us look at some of the important reasons as to why discipline is superior to motivation.

DURATION

Being disciplined is a state of mind. Hence, it exists for a longer duration. On the other hand, motivation is more of a thought and is often based on the situation. You may be motivated to do a certain task today. That doesn't imply that you will be motivated to do the same task tomorrow.

Motivation does not exist in a uniform manner at all times. You may be highly motivated now, but you might lack in motivation during the rest of the day. However, disciplining your mind is an ongoing process and does not vary drastically. For example, if you are disciplined to hit the gym every day for an hour, you will do it no matter what!

STABILITY

Discipline is more stable and is capable of helping you change your lifestyle in the long run. It will help you to make incremental changes to your life and get rewarded in the process. On the other hand, your motivation levels can be compared to the effects of consuming a drug. You feel extremely motivated at the beginning of the day. As the hours fly, your motivation levels also keep fluctuating drastically. Some of us need external stimuli to even get motivated at times. But, once you discipline your mind, it doesn't have to be probed any further.

IMPACT

The impact of motivation is only short lived. You would appreciate the impact of motivation only for the time being, while it still lasts. For example, you lack the motivation to go to work. You will then look for an external stimulus to motivate you to get out of bed and get ready for work. The effects of the motivation are no longer felt or appreciated, the moment you reach office.

As I already mentioned before, the benefits of self-discipline are capable of changing your life and can be felt in the long run too. Hence, disciplining yourself has a greater impact than being motivated.

In other words, self-discipline is more effective in helping you improve your lifestyle than motivation.

ENERGY REQUIRED

In the case of motivation, sometimes we require external stimuli to get started. So, a good amount of our energies will be spent trying to motivate ourselves. Once motivated, the rest of the energy will be spent towards completing the task. When you constantly rely on motivation to start your work, you feel handicapped and unproductive, in the absence of an external stimulus. This has an impact on the quality of your work as well as your productivity.

On the other hand, self-discipline trains your mind and body to function in a certain way. For example, you may discipline your mind to do a set of tasks as soon as you wake up. When this discipline exists, you don't need any kind of motivation to carry out these tasks. You will automatically be spending your energy and effort on completing these tasks.

In other words, being motivated takes up a lot more energy than being disciplined.

PROMOTING CONSISTENCY

As I already mentioned, motivation is a temporary emotion. When you rely on motivation to commence your work, there will be times when you abstain from working, just because you don't feel like it. In the absence of any motivating factors, you will not be mentally prepared to undertake any activity. If you are forced to work on something, despite lacking the motivation to do so, the quality of your work will be severely impacted. You will not be able to apply your efforts in a consistent manner.

On the other hand, if you are self-disciplined, you will be able to focus on your work, irrespective of your state of mind. Your efforts will be channelized in a consistent manner, irrespective of how motivated you feel to work. Thus, being disciplined, helps in ensuring that your productivity levels are not affected and the quality of your work is not compromised. To put it in simpler terms, you will be solely dependent on your mind or rather, your discipline to guide you and not look for any external stimuli to make you focus on work.

It is because of the consistency element, you need to be disciplined first before you look for motivation. There may be situations in life, where no matter how hard you try, you will not be motivated, but you still must deliver your best. In such circumstances, if your mind is already disciplined to take action, you will be able to handle the situation in a calm and composed manner, without having to worry about motivational factors.

SUSTAINABILITY

You will be able to sustain your self-discipline for a longer period of time. In fact, once you discipline your body and mind to behave in a certain way, unless you decide to change it, you will be able to sustain your state of mind. Your self-discipline will help you sustain your energy levels as well, since your efforts will be more channelized and efficient. Hence, self-discipline is more of a self-fueling system.

On the other hand, motivation is a short-lived phenomenon. You will have to expend a lot of energy and rely on so many other factors, to stay motivated at all times. Hence, motivation becomes difficult to sustain over a longer duration.

These are some of the important reasons why self-discipline is far superior to motivation! You become a self-sufficient individual, when you are disciplined!

CONCLUSION

That brings us to the end of this book! I know that was a lot of information to process in such a short span of time. Embarking on the journey of disciplining your mind and body can be quite a daunting task. You will feel discouraged midway! But, remember the positive effects of discipline on your life. Imagine how you can improve your life, by adding some discipline to it. This will definitely encourage you to keep trying until you fully incorporate discipline as part of your lifestyle!

I sincerely hope that you found this book useful. I wish you all the best in this journey towards disciplining your life.

Thank you and good luck!